LOOK ■ AROUND ■ YOU

THE HOMES WE LIVE IN

Sally Hewitt and Jane Rowe

Evans

Evans Brothers Limited

About this book

This book has been put together in a way that makes it ideal for teachers and parents to share with young children. Take time over each question and project. Have fun learning about how all sorts of different homes, and the objects in them, have been designed for a special purpose.

The Homes We Live In deals with the kinds of ideas about design and technology that many children will be introduced to in their early years at school. The pictures and text will encourage children to explore design on the page, and all around them. This will help them to understand why their homes, furniture and decorations are made from particular materials, have a certain shape, size and pattern, and work well. It will also help them develop their own design skills.

The 'Eye-opener' boxes reveal interesting and unusual facts, or lead children to examine one aspect of design. There are also activities that put theory into practice in an entertaining and informative way. Children learn most effectively by joining in, talking, asking questions and solving problems, so encourage them to talk about what they are doing and to find ways of solving the problems for themselves.

Try to make thinking about design and technology a part of everyday life. Just pick any object around the house and talk about why it has been made that way, and how it could be improved. Design is not just a subject for adults. You can have a lot of fun with it at any age – and develop both artistic flair and practical skills.

Contents

The homes we live in

What is a home?
Your home is where you live with your family.

It shelters you from the weather.

You feel safe there.

It is where you keep all your things and play with your friends.

Architects design the buildings we live in, but homes are not just buildings.

You can choose furniture, pictures, colours and patterns to make a building into your own special place.

This book will show you all kinds of homes and why they have been designed in a certain way.

All kinds of homes

People live in all kinds of different homes.

▲ Joanne and Ellie are neighbours. They live on either side of the same wall that joins their houses together.

▲ Bobby lives in a big house with a garden where he can play.

▶ Nick goes up in a lift to his apartment on the fifth floor of this building.

What kind of home do you live in?

Some people have mobile homes. They can drive their home wherever they want to go.

Why do you think a mobile home is made of light materials?

Make a collage

Collect and cut out pictures of homes from all around the world to make your own collage.

Look at all the different shapes and materials that they are made from.

Outside

Homes built to last for a long time are made of strong materials.

▶ Bricks are all the same size and shape so that they are easy to build with.

Wood is light and strong.
It can be painted or varnished to protect it from the weather.

Cement fixes bricks together like strong glue.

▲ Why is glass a good material for windows?

Build a strong wall

Find some toy bricks all the same shape and size.

▶ Build a wall in this pattern. Tap a brick near the middle of the bottom row sharply with a pencil. What happens?

tap here

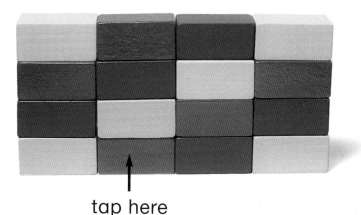

tap here

◀ Now do the same to a wall in this pattern. Which one makes the strongest wall?

How many different materials can you see in this picture?

Look at the outside of your home.

What different materials and patterns can you find?

Roofs

Roofs protect the inside of houses from all kinds of weather.

gutter

▶ Sloping roofs like this are called pitched roofs. Rain, snow and leaves slide off and collect in the gutter.

◀ When rain falls on the flat roof of some apartment blocks it runs down, through a pipe, to the drains below.

Eye-opener

Homes in very dry places often have flat roofs. Why do you think this is?

Make a mini roof

Roof tiles overlap in a pattern that is rather like the scales of a fish.

Try the experiment below to find out why.

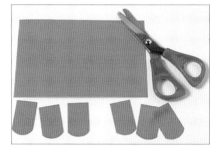 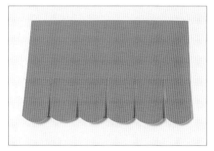 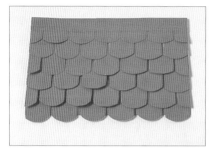

1 Cut out a rectangle and some tiles from shiny card.

2 Glue the first row of tiles along the bottom edge of the rectangle.

3 Glue the other rows so that the tiles overlap in a fish-scale pattern.

 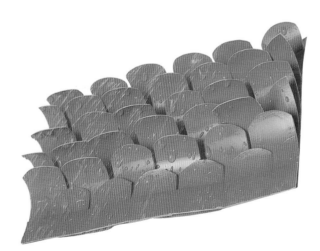

4 Pour water down over the tiles like rain.
What happens?

5 Now turn the card upside down and pour water over it.
What happens now?

Doors

You go in and out of your home through your front door.

How many doors are there inside your home?
Is there a door for every room?

A door is attached to a door frame by hinges so that you can swing it open and shut easily.

Why do you think doors are usually this shape and size?

Look how difficult these funny-shaped doors are to walk through.

Your front door is the strongest door in your home.
You can lock it shut.

It needs a handle to open it.
It needs a letter box and a name or a number for the mail. It needs a knocker or bell for visitors.

Eye-opener

Some front doors have a peephole. You can see who is calling, but the caller cannot see you.

Door handles must be the right shape for your hand.

Which of these handles is the right shape for turning?
Which one is designed for pushing down?
Which one is designed for pulling?

Windows

Imagine your home without any windows. It would probably be very dark and stuffy!

Is there a room in your house that you think doesn't need windows?

▼ This is a sash window with a wooden frame.

The top and the bottom parts can slide up or down to open and shut.

▲ What do windows look like on the inside?

Some have curtains that can be drawn. Do you think curtains make a room cooler or warmer?

16

You can also put blinds on a window.

These 'venetian' blinds are made of thin strips of metal.
The strips can be turned so that they let in the light or keep it out.

Would you rather have curtains or blinds in your bedroom?

Having fun with light

Coverings can change the way light comes through windows.

1 Make a frame from some card.
2 Blu-tack different materials to the frame, one at a time.
3 Try each one out by propping the frame against the window when the sun is shining.

Which material lets in most light?
Which material lets in no light?
Which can you see through?

If you use paper and cut shapes in it, what happens then?

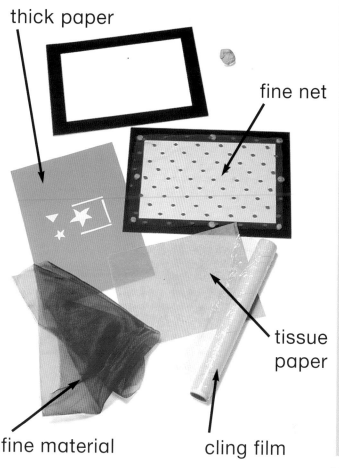

thick paper

fine net

tissue paper

fine material

cling film

Up and down

Stairs are designed for you to go up and down between floors.

Some people have short legs and some have long legs.

Some people have big feet and some have little feet.

Stairs have to be designed for everyone to use, whatever the size of their legs and feet.

Why do you think stairs have banisters?

Ordinary stairs slope from top to bottom.

A spiral staircase curls round and round. When you reach the top, you are directly above the place where you started.

Would it be easy to carry a big box up spiral stairs?

Eye-opener

A stair-lift carries people who find it difficult to walk up and down stairs.

What other ways can you go up and down inside buildings without using stairs?

Look on page 30 to check your answers.

Inside

What are the floors of your home covered with?
Do they feel soft or smooth? How do you keep them clean?

▲ Carpets and rugs make the floor soft and comfortable. They help to keep your house warm.

◀ Wood can be sanded and polished to make smooth, shiny floors.

▶ Tiles protect walls and are easy to wipe clean. You need a lot of them to cover a whole wall. Which rooms would you have tiles in?

One big pot of paint can cover the walls of a whole room!

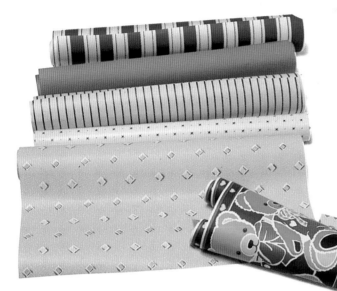

You can use rolls of wallpaper to decorate your walls with colours and patterns.

Design your own wallpaper

A stencil can be used again and again to create a pattern.

1 Cut shapes out of pieces of card.

2 Now put your stencil down onto clean paper and sponge on some coloured paint.

3 Lift the stencil carefully and do it again.

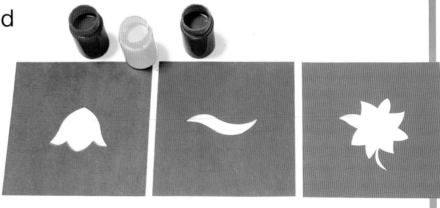

Furniture

Just a bed and a wardrobe will turn
an empty room into a bedroom.

Think about how you would use
the furniture on these pages.
Where would you put them in your home?

These tables look very different.

Which one would you do your homework on?

Could all these things be stored on these shelves?

What would you like to keep on the shelves?

Where would you put the shelves in your home?

Eye-opener

This chair doesn't take up much room at all.

You can also fold it out into a long chair that you can lie on, or make it totally flat, to form a bed.

Why might you buy one of these instead of an ordinary bed?

Decoration

It's not difficult to guess what Millie and Nick's favourite colours are.

Millie wants to decorate her bedroom in her favourite colour.

Would Nick's favourite colours be good for decorating his room?

Would your favourite colour look good in your room?
If not, which room in your house would it suit?

Collect lots of coloured things.
Pick objects like the ones in
this picture or choose paper,
toys, jewellery and clothes.

Put colours together
in different ways to
find out which ones
you think go together
well.

People often pick
a certain subject,
called a theme,
for a room.

What theme do
these decorations
have? Which room
would you put
them in?

What is your favourite theme?
Draw some things you might have in your room
if it had that theme.

The right temperature

A well-designed home keeps you warm when it is cold outside and cool when it is hot outside.

People have always sat around a fire to keep warm.

Fireplaces have to be built from fireproof materials. Smoke escapes safely up the chimney.

▶ Hot water fills a radiator to make it feel warm.

Fires and radiators are usually in the middle of the wall so that the heat can spread all around the room.

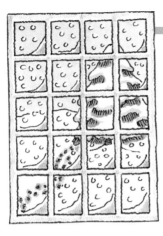

▶ A breeze coming through an open window can keep a room cooler on a hot day.

▼ A fan can make a cool breeze when the weather is hot and still.

Bricks, glass and other materials help to keep your home warm or cool.

Feel the walls, floors and windows in your home.
Why do you think they feel different temperatures?

Eye-opener

The Ancient Romans knew all about central heating. Their floors were raised on pillars. Hot air from a big fire passed under the floor and warmed up the room above.

Amazing designs

People live in these houses and use this furniture, but look how imaginative the designers have been with their ideas!

Outside

▶ The general design of these homes is based on one particular shape.
Do you know which shape it is?

▼ The roof of this amazing house contains a special 'insulating' material. This helps to keep it a pleasant temperature inside all the time.

Inside

▲ Would you like knobs like this on your furniture? What other ideas for knobs can you think of?

▲ What is unusual about this kitchen?

◀ This table and chair are made of cardboard. When you buy them they are folded flat. You unfold them and decorate them any way you like.

All answers are on page 30.

Index

Answers to pages 19, 28 and 29

Page 19/Eye-Opener box: Lifts and escalators

Page 28: The first house is based on cube shapes

Page 29: Everything about this kitchen is curved in some way